DC

HEAL TODAY?

Booklets taken from *Alpha: Questions of Life:*

Christianity:Boring, Untrue and Irrelevant?
Who Is Jesus?
Why Did Jesus Die?
How Can I Be Sure of My Faith?
Why and How Should I Read the Bible?
Why and How Do I Pray?
How Does God Guide Us?
The Holy Spirit
How Can I Resist Evil?
Why and How Should We Tell Others?
Does God Heal Today?
What About the Church?
How Can I Make the Most of the Rest of My Life?

Booklets taken from *Searching Issues:*

Why Does God Allow Suffering?
What About Other Religions?
Is There Anything Wrong With Sex Before Marriage?
How Does the New Age Movement Relate to Christianity?
What Is the Christian Attitude to Homosexuality?
Is There a Conflict Between Science and Christianity?
Is the Trinity Unbiblical, Unbelievable and Irrelevant?

Does God Heal Today?

NICKY GUMBEL

Alpha

Text cartoons by Charlie Mackesy
Cover artwork by Glenn Andrews

ISBN 1 84291 192 9

Published by
KINGSWAY COMMUNICATIONS LTD
Lottbridge Drove, Eastbourne BN23 6NT, England.
Email: books@kingsway.co.uk
Printed in Canada.

Contents

Does God Heal Today?

A few years ago, a Japanese girl asked myself and my wife to pray for her back problem to be healed. We placed our hands on her and asked God to heal her. Thereafter, I tried to avoid bumping into her because I was not sure how to explain to her why she had not been healed. One day she came round the corner and I could not avoid her. I thought it only polite to ask the dreaded question, 'How is your back?'

'Oh,' she replied, 'it was completely healed after you prayed for it.'

I don't know why I was so surprised, but I was.

When John Wimber came to our church with a team from his church (the Vineyard Christian Fellowship), he preached one Sunday on the subject of healing. On Monday he came to a gathering of leaders. There were about sixty or seventy of us in the room and he spoke again about healing. We had heard talks on healing before, and felt quite happy about what he said on the subject. That was until he said that we were going to break for coffee and then have a 'workshop'. We were now on unfamiliar ground. John Wimber said that his team had had some twelve 'words of knowledge' about the people in the room. He told us that by a 'word of knowledge' (1 Corinthians 12:8) he meant a supernatural revelation of facts concerning a person or a situation, which is not learned by the efforts of the natural mind, but is made known by the Spirit of God. This may be in the form of a picture, a word seen or heard in the mind, or a feeling experienced physically. He then gave a whole list of them and said that he was going to invite people to come forward to be prayed for. I, for one, was most sceptical about the whole event.

However, as one by one the people responded to some of the quite detailed descriptions (my recollection is that one of them was for 'a man who had injured his back chopping wood when he was fourteen'), the level of faith in the room began to rise. Every word of knowledge was responded to. One of them concerned sterility. We all knew each other well and felt sure that this was not applicable to anyone in the group. However, a girl who had been unable to conceive, bravely went forward. She was prayed for and had her first of five children exactly nine months later!

My attitude during that evening reflects the fear and scepticism many of us in the twenty-first century bring to the subject of healing. I decided to reread the Bible to try to understand what it said about healing. Of course, God heals with the co-operation of doctors, nurses and the whole medical profession. But the more I have looked, the more convinced I am that we should also expect God to heal miraculously today.

HEALING IN THE BIBLE

In the Old Testament we find God's promises to bring healing and health to his people if they obey him (eg, Exodus 23:25–26; Deuteronomy 28; Psalm 41). Indeed, it is in his character to heal, for he says, 'I am the Lord who heals you' (Exodus 15:26). We also find several examples of miraculous healing (eg, 1 Kings 13:6; 2 Kings 4:8–37; Isaiah 38).

One of the most striking examples is the healing of Naaman, the commander of the army of the King of Aram, who had leprosy. God healed him after he had reluctantly dipped himself seven times in the River Jordan. 'His flesh was restored and became clean like that of a young boy' (2 Kings 5:14), and he recognised the God of Israel to be the only true God. Elisha, who had instructed him, refused the payment which Naaman offered (although his servant Gehazi made the fatal mistake of trying, deceitfully, to get money for himself as a result of the healing). We see, first, from this story that healing can have a remarkable effect on a person's life – not just physically, but also in their relationship with God. Healing and faith can go hand in hand. Secondly, if God acted in this way in the Old Testament, when there were only glimpses of the kingdom of God and the outpouring of the Spirit, we can confidently expect that he will do so, even more, now that Jesus has inaugurated the kingdom of God and the age of the Spirit.

The first recorded words of Jesus in Mark's Gospel are, 'The time has come … The kingdom of God is near. Repent and believe the good news!' (Mark 1:15). The theme of the kingdom of God is central to the ministry of Jesus. The expressions 'the kingdom of God' and 'the kingdom of heaven' are used more than eighty-two times, although the latter is confined to Matthew's Gospel. The two terms are synonymous.

'Heaven' was a common Jewish expression for referring to God without mentioning the divine name. The Jewish background to Matthew's Gospel, as opposed to the Gentile orientation of Luke and Mark, probably explains the different use.

The Greek word for 'kingdom', *basileia*, is a translation of the Aramaic *malkuth*, which was in all probability the expression that Jesus used. It means not only 'kingdom' in the sense of a political or geographical realm, but also carries the notion of activity – the activity of ruling or reigning. Thus 'the kingdom of God' means 'the rule and reign of God'.

In the teaching of Jesus, the kingdom of God has a future aspect which will only be fulfilled with a decisive event at 'the end of the age' (Matthew 13:49). For example, in one of the parables of the kingdom, he speaks of a coming harvest at the end of the age when 'the Son of Man … will weed out of his kingdom everything that causes sin and all who do evil … Then the righteous will shine like the sun in the kingdom of their Father' (Matthew 13:24–43). The end of the age will come when Jesus returns. When he came the first time, he came in weakness; when he returns, he will come 'with power and great glory' (Matthew 24:30).

History is moving towards this climax with the glorious coming of Jesus Christ (Matthew 25:31). In all, there are over 300 references in the New Testament to the second coming of Christ. When he returns it will be obvious to all. History, as we know it, will end. There will be a universal resurrection and a Day of Judgement. For some (those who reject Christ), it will be a day of destruction (2 Thessalonians 1:8–9); for others, it will be a day of receiving their inheritance in the kingdom of God (Matthew 25:34). There will be a new heaven and a new earth (2 Peter 3:13; Revelation 21:1). Jesus himself will be there

(Revelation 21:22–23) and so will all who love and obey him. It will be a place of intense happiness which goes on for ever (1 Corinthians 2:9). We shall have new bodies which are imperishable and glorious (1 Corinthians 15:42–43). There will be no more death or mourning or crying or pain (Revelation 21:4). All who believe will be totally healed on that day.

On the other hand, there is a present aspect to the kingdom of God in the teaching and activity of Jesus. We see the signs, the dawning, the budding of the approaching kingdom. Jesus told the Pharisees, 'The kingdom of God is among you' (Luke 17:20–21). In his parable of the hidden treasure and the pearl (Matthew 13:44–46), Jesus suggests that the kingdom is something which can be discovered and experienced in this age. Throughout the Gospels it is clear that Jesus saw his ministry as the fulfilment of the Old Testament promises in history. In the synagogue at Nazareth, Jesus read the prophecy from Isaiah 61:1–2 and asserted, 'Today this scripture is fulfilled in your hearing' (Luke 4:21). He went on to demonstrate this present reality of the kingdom by all that he did during his ministry, in the forgiveness of sins, the suppression of evil and the healing of the sick.

The kingdom is both 'now' and 'not yet'. The Jewish expectation was that the Messiah would immediately inaugurate a completed kingdom, as shown in the diagram below:

THIS AGE   **AGE TO COME**

Jesus' teaching was a modification of this and can be summarised in the following diagram:

The age to come
realised in principle   AGE TO COME

First coming of Jesus

Second coming of Jesus

The period
in which we
now live

THIS AGE

We live between the times, when the age to come has
broken into history. The old age goes on, but the powers of the
new age have erupted into this age. The future kingdom has
broken into history. Jesus preached the kingdom of God. He
also demonstrated its breaking into history by healing the sick,
raising the dead and driving out demons.

A quarter of the Gospels is concerned with healing.
Although Jesus did not heal all in Judea who were sick, we
often read of him healing either individuals or groups of people
(eg, Matthew 4:23; 9:35; Mark 6:56; Luke 4:40; 6:19; 9:11). It
was part of the normal activity of the kingdom.

Not only did he do this himself, but he commissioned his
disciples to do the same. First, he commissioned the twelve.
This is clearly set out in Matthew's Gospel. Matthew tells us
that 'Jesus went throughout Galilee, teaching in their synagogues, preaching the good news of the kingdom, and healing
every disease and sickness among the people' (Matthew 4:23).
He then gives some of the teaching and preaching of Jesus in

Matthew 5–7 (the Sermon on the Mount), then nine miracles (mainly of healing) and he concludes with an almost exact repetition of Matthew 4:23: 'Jesus went through all the towns and villages, teaching in their synagogues, preaching the good news of the kingdom and healing every kind of disease and sickness' (Matthew 9:35). Matthew is using a literary device of repetition known as an *inclusio*, which was used instead of punctuation and the breaking up of the text with paragraphs to indicate the beginning and end of a section. Having shown what Jesus himself did, Matthew tells us that Jesus then sent the twelve out to do the same. He told them to go out and preach the same message: ' "The kingdom of heaven is near." Heal the sick, raise the dead, cleanse those who have leprosy, drive out demons …' (Matthew 10:8).

Nor was it only the twelve to whom he gave this commission. There was also a further group of seventy-two whom he appointed. He told them to go out and 'heal the sick … and tell them, "The kingdom of God is near you" ' (Luke 10:9). They returned with joy and said, 'Lord, even the demons submit to us in your name' (v. 17).

Nor were his commissions confined to the twelve and the seventy-two. Jesus expected *all* his disciples to do the same. He told his disciples to 'go and make disciples of all nations … teaching them to obey *everything* I have commanded you' (Matthew 28:18–20, italics mine). He did not say, 'Everything except, of course, the healing bit.'

We find the same in the longer ending of Mark's Gospel (which is, at least, very good evidence of what the early church understood Jesus' commission to be). Jesus said, ' "Go into all the world and preach the good news to all creation … and these signs will accompany *those who believe*: In my name they will drive out demons … they will place their hands on sick people, and they will get well" … Then the disciples went out and preached everywhere, and the Lord worked with them and confirmed his word by the signs that accompanied it' (Mark 16:15–20, italics mine). Jesus says, 'These signs will accompany *those who believe*' – that is to say those 'who believe' in Jesus Christ, which means all Christians.

We find the same in John's Gospel. Jesus said, in the context of miracles, 'Anyone who has faith in me will do what I have been doing. He will do even greater things than these, because I am going to the Father' (John 14:12). Clearly no one has performed miracles of greater quality than Jesus, but there has been a greater quantity since Jesus returned to the Father. He has not ceased to perform miracles, but he now uses weak and imperfect human beings. Again it is 'anyone who has faith in me'. That is you and me. These commands and promises are not restricted anywhere to a special category of Christians.

Jesus healed; he told his disciples to do the same and they did so. In the Book of Acts we see the working out of this commission. The disciples continued to preach and teach, but also to heal the sick, raise the dead and cast out demons (Acts 3:1–10; 4:12; 5:12–16; 8:5–13; 9:32–43; 14:3, 8–10; 19:11–12; 20:9–12; 28:8–9). It is clear from 1 Corinthians 12–14 that Paul did not believe that such abilities were confined to the apostles. Likewise, the writer to the Hebrews says that God testified to his message by 'signs, wonders and various miracles, and gifts of the Holy Spirit' (Hebrews 2:4).

Nowhere in the Bible does it say that healing was confined to any particular period of history. On the contrary, healing is one of the signs of the kingdom which was inaugurated by Jesus Christ and continues to this day. We should expect God to continue to heal miraculously today as part of his kingdom activity.

HEALING IN CHURCH HISTORY

In her book *Christian Healing* Evelyn Frost examined in detail passages of early church writers, such as Quadratus, Justin Martyr, Theophilus of Antioch, Irenaeus, Tertullian and Origen, and concluded that healing formed a normal part of the activity of the early church.

Irenaeus (c. 130–c. 200) who was Bishop of Lyons and one of the theologians of the early church wrote:

> Those who are in truth his disciples, receiving grace from him, do in his name perform [miracles], so as to promote the welfare of other men, according to the gift which each one has received from him. For some do certainly and truly drive out devils, so that those who have thus been cleansed from evil spirits frequently both believe [in Christ], and join themselves to the church. Others have foreknowledge of things to come: they see visions, and utter prophetic expressions. Others still, heal the sick by laying their hands upon them and they are made whole. Yea, moreover, as I have said, the dead have been raised up, and remain among us for many years. (*Against Heresies* II, Ch. XXXII)

Origen (c. 185–c. 254), another theologian, biblical scholar and writer of the early church, said of Christians: 'They expel evil spirits, and perform many cures, and foresee certain events … the name of Jesus … can take away diseases.'

Two hundred years later there was still an expectation that God would heal people directly. Augustine of Hippo (AD 354–430), whom many regard as the greatest theologian of the first four centuries, says in his book *The City of God* that '*even now* miracles are wrought in the name of Christ'. He cites the example of a blind man's sight restored in Milan, when he was there. He then describes the cure of a man he was staying with, called Innocentius. He was being treated by the doctors for fistulae, of which he had 'a large number intricately seated in the rectum'! He had undergone one very painful operation. It was not thought that he would survive another operation. While they were praying for him he was cast down to the ground as if someone had hurled him violently to the earth, groaning and sobbing, his whole body shaking so that he could not speak. The dreaded day for the next operation came. 'The surgeons arrived … the frightful instruments are produced … the part is bared; the surgeon … with knife in hand, eagerly looks for the sinus that is to be cut. He searches for it with his eyes; he feels for it with his finger; he applies every kind of scrutiny.' He found a perfectly healed wound. 'No words of mine can describe the joy, and praise, and thanksgiving to the merciful and almighty God which was poured from the lips of all, with tears and gladness. Let the scene be imagined rather than described!'

Next he described the healing of Innocentia – a devout woman of the highest rank in the state – who was healed of what the doctors described as incurable breast cancer. The doctor was curious to find out how she had been healed. When she told him that Jesus had healed her, he was furious and said, 'I thought you would make some great discovery to me.' She, shuddering at the indifference, quickly replied, 'What great thing was it for Christ to heal a cancer, who raised one who had been four days dead?'

He goes on to tell of a doctor with gout who was healed in the 'very act of baptism' and an old comedian who was also cured at baptism, not only of paralysis, but also of a hernia. Augustine says he knows of so many miraculous healings that he says at one point, 'What am I to do? I am so pressed by the promise of finishing this work, that I cannot record all the miracles I know … even now, therefore many miracles are wrought, the same God, who wrought those we read of, still performing them, by whom he will and as he will.'

All the way through church history God has continued to heal people directly. There has never been a time when healing has died out – right up to the present day.

Edward Gibbon, the English rationalist, historian and scholar, best known as the author of *The History of the Decline and Fall of the Roman Empire* (1776–1788), lists five causes for the remarkable and rapid growth of Christianity. One of these is 'the miraculous powers of the primitive Church'. He says, 'The Christian Church, from the time of the apostles and their first disciples has claimed an uninterrupted succession of miraculous powers, the gift of tongues, of vision and of prophecy, the power of expelling demons, of healing the sick and of raising the dead.' Gibbon goes on to point out the inconsistency of his own day when 'a latent, and even involuntary, scepticism adheres to the most pious dispositions'. By contrast to the early church, he writes that in the church of his day 'admission of supernatural truths is much less an active consent than a cold and placid acquiescence. Accustomed long since to observe and to respect the invariable order of Nature, our reason, or at least our imagination, is not sufficiently prepared to sustain the visible action of the Deity.' The same could be said even more so of our own day.

HEALING TODAY

God is still healing people today. There are so many wonderful stories of God healing that it is difficult to know which to give as an example. Ajay Gohill told his story at a recent baptism and confirmation service at our church. He was born in Kenya and came to England in 1971. He had been brought up as a Hindu and worked in his family business as a newsagent in Neasden. At the age of twenty-one he contracted erythrodermic psoriasis, a chronic skin disease. His weight dropped from 11.5 to 7.5 stone. He was treated all over the world – in the United States, Germany, Switzerland, Israel and all over England, including Harley Street. He said that he spent 80 per cent of his earnings on trying to find a cure. He took strong drugs which affected his liver. Eventually, he had to give up his job. The disease was all over his body from head to toe. He was so horrible to look at that he could not go swimming or even wear a T-shirt. He lost all his friends. His wife and son left him. He wanted to die. On 20 August 1987 he was in a wheelchair in the Elizabeth Ward of St Thomas' Hospital. He spent over seven weeks in hospital receiving various kinds of treatments. On 14 October he was lying in his bed and wanted to die. He cried out, 'God, if you are watching, let me die – I am sorry if I have done something wrong.' He said that as he prayed he 'felt a presence'. He looked in his locker and pulled out a Good News Bible. He opened it at random and read Psalm 38:

> O Lord, don't punish me in your anger! You have wounded me with your arrows; you have struck me down. Because of your anger, I am in great pain; my whole body is diseased because of my sins. I am drowning in the flood of my sins; they are a burden too heavy to bear. Because I have been foolish, my sores stink and rot. I am bowed down, I am crushed; I mourn all day long. I am

burning with fever and I am near to death. I am worn out and utterly crushed; my heart is troubled, and I groan with pain. O Lord, you know what I long for; you hear all my groans. My heart is pounding, my strength is gone, and my eyes have lost their brightness. My friends and neighbours will not come near me, because of my sores; even my family keeps away from me ... Do not abandon me, O Lord; do not stay away, my God! Help me now, O Lord my saviour! (Psalm 38:1–11, 21–22, GNB).

Each and every verse seemed relevant to him. He prayed for God to heal him and fell into a deep sleep. When he awoke the next morning 'everything looked new'. He went to the bathroom and relaxed in a bath. As he looked at the bathwater, he saw his skin had lifted off and was floating in the bath. He called the nurses in and told them that God was healing him. All his skin was new like a baby's. He had been totally healed. Since then he has been reunited with his son. He says that the inner healing that has taken place in his life is even greater than the physical healing. He says, 'Every day I live for Jesus. I am his servant today.'

God is a God who heals. The Greek word which means 'I save' also means 'I heal'. God is concerned not just about our spiritual salvation, but also about our whole being. One day we shall have a new perfect body but in this life we will never reach perfection. When God heals someone miraculously today we get a glimpse of the future when the final redemption of our bodies will take place (Romans 8:23). Of course not everyone we pray for will necessarily be healed and no human being can ultimately avoid death. Our bodies are decaying. At some point it may even be right to prepare a person for death rather than praying for their healing. Indeed, the love and concern shown to people who are dying, for example, by the hospice movement, gives dignity to the terminally ill and is another out-working of Jesus' commission to care for the sick. So we need to be sensitive to the guidance of the Holy Spirit.

This should not discourage us from praying for people to be healed. The more people we pray for, the more we shall see healed. Those who are not healed usually speak of the blessing of being prayed for – provided they are prayed for with love and sensitivity. I remember a group of us at theological college praying for a man with a bad back. I don't think he was healed, but he said to me afterwards, 'This is the first time since I have been at theological college that I felt anyone cared.' Another man said to me recently that although he had not been healed when he was prayed for, he had had his greatest experience ever of the Spirit of God, and his life has been transformed.

Some are given special gifts of healing (1 Corinthians 12:9). Today, around the world, we find examples of those with an extraordinary gift of healing. This does not mean that we can leave it all to them. The commission to heal is for all of us. Just as we do not all have the gift of evangelism, but we are all called to tell others about Jesus, so we do not all have the gift of healing, but we are all called to pray for the sick.

How in practice do we go about praying for the sick? It is vital to remember that it is God who heals, not us. There is no technique involved. We pray with love and simplicity. The motivation of Jesus was his compassion for people (Mark 1:41; Matthew 9:36). If we love people we will always treat them with respect and dignity. If we believe it is Jesus who heals we will pray with simplicity, because it is not our prayer but the power of God that brings healing.

Here is a simple pattern:

Where does it hurt?

We ask the person who wants prayer for healing what is wrong and what they would like us to pray for.

Why does the person have this condition?

Of course, a leg broken in a car accident will be obvious, but at other times we may need to ask God to show us if there is a root cause to the problem. One woman in our congregation had developed backache with pain in her left hip, which interfered with sleep, movement and work. The doctor prescribed pills for arthritis. She asked for prayer one evening. The girl who was praying for her said that the word 'forgiveness' had come to her mind. After a struggle the woman was able to forgive somebody who had wronged her, and she was partially healed. She was totally healed at the moment she posted a forgiving letter to her friend.

How do I pray?

There are various models in the New Testament which we follow. They are all simple. Sometimes we pray for God to heal in the name of Jesus and we ask the Holy Spirit to come on the person. Prayer may be accompanied by anointing with oil (James 5:14). More often it is accompanied by the laying on of hands (Luke 4:40).

How are they feeling?

After we have prayed we usually ask the person what they are experiencing. Sometimes they feel nothing – in which case we continue to pray. At other times they feel that they are healed, although time alone will tell. On other occasions they feel better but are not totally healed, in which case we continue as

Jesus did with the blind man (Mark 8:22–25). We continue praying until we feel it is right to stop.

What next?

After praying for healing it is important to reassure people of God's love for them regardless of whether they are healed or not, and to give them the liberty to come back and be prayed for again. We must avoid putting burdens on people, such as suggesting that it is their lack of faith that has prevented healing from taking place. We always encourage people to go on praying and to ensure that their lives are rooted in the healing community of the church – which is the place where long-term healing so often occurs.

Finally, it is important to persist in praying for people to be healed. It is easy to get discouraged, especially if we do not see immediate dramatic results. We continue because of our obedience to the calling and commission from Jesus Christ to preach the kingdom and to demonstrate its coming by, among other things, healing the sick. If we persist over the years we will see God healing people.

I was once asked to visit a woman in the Brompton Hospital. She was in her thirties, had three children and was pregnant with a fourth. Her common-law husband had left her and she was on her own. Her third child, who was a Down's syndrome child, had a hole in his heart which had been operated on. The operation had not been a success and, not unnaturally, the medical staff wanted to turn the machines off. Three times they asked her if they could turn the machines off and let the baby die. She said no, as she wanted to try one last thing. She wanted someone to pray for him. So I came, and she told me that she didn't believe in God, but she showed me her son. He had tubes all over him and his body was bruised and swollen. She said that the doctors had indicated that even if he recovered he would have brain damage because his heart had stopped for such a long time. She said, 'Will you pray?' So I prayed in the name of Jesus for God to heal him. Then I explained to her how she could give her life to Jesus Christ and she did that. I left, but returned two days later. She came running out the moment she saw me. She said, 'I've been trying to get hold of you: something amazing has happened. The night after you prayed he completely turned the corner. He has recovered.' Within a few days he had gone home. I tried to keep in contact with her, but didn't know where she lived, although she kept leaving messages on the phone. About six months later I was in the lift in another hospital and saw a mother and child whom I did not recognise at once. The woman said, 'Are you Nicky?' I said, 'Yes.' She said, 'That is the little boy you prayed for. It is amazing. Not only has he recovered from the operation, but his hearing, which was bad beforehand, is better. He still has Down's syndrome, but he is much better than he was before.'

Since then I have taken two funerals for other members of that family. At each of them people have come up to me, none of them churchgoers, saying, 'You were the person who prayed for Craig to be healed and God healed him.' They all believe that God healed him, because they know that he was dying. The change in Vivienne, the child's mother, had also made a deep impression on them. She was so changed after coming to Christ that she decided to marry the person with whom she was living. He had come back to her after seeing the change in her life. They are now married and she is totally transformed. On the second occasion, Vivienne went round all the relatives and friends saying, 'I didn't believe, but now I do believe.' Not long afterwards, Craig's uncle and aunt came to church, sat in the front row and gave their lives to Jesus Christ. They did so because they knew they had seen God's power in healing.

Study Guide

1. What would you say to someone who shows *'fear and scepticism'* over the question of healing? (p. 8)

2. What does Nicky mean by the *'now'* and *'not yet'* of the kingdom of God (p. 11)? How can understanding this help us in thinking about healing?

3. How would you answer someone who claimed that Jesus' command to his disciples that they should heal the sick no longer applies to us today (p. 13)?

4. *'Not everyone we pray for will necessarily be healed'* (p. 19). Why not? Does this matter?

5. Why is it important to *'pray with simplicity'* (p. 20)? What are the practical steps that Nicky recommends?

6. What would say to someone who thought that healing had not taken place because the person concerned did not have enough faith (p. 22)?

7. Why is it important to persist in praying for healing, even when *'we do not see immediate, dramatic results'* (p. 22)?

Alpha

This book is an Alpha resource. The Alpha course is a practical introduction to the Christian faith initiated by Holy Trinity Brompton in London, and now being run by thousands of churches throughout the UK as well as overseas.

For more information on Alpha, and details of tapes, videos and training manuals, contact the Alpha office, Holy Trinity Brompton on 0207 581 8255, (home page: http://www.alphacourse.org), or STL, PO Box 300, Kingstown Broadway, Carlisle, Cumbria CA3 0QS.

Alpha Hotline for telephone orders:
0845 7581 278 (all calls at local rate)

To order from overseas:
Tel +44 1228 611749
Fax +44 1228 514949

Email: alpha@stl.org

Alpha

Alpha titles available

Alpha: Questions of Life   The Alpha course in book form. In fifteen compelling chapters Nicky Gumbel points the way to an authentic Christianity which is exciting and relevant to todays world.

Searching Issues   The seven issues most often raised by participants on the Alpha course: suffering, other religions, sex before marriage, the New Age, homosexuality, science and Christianity, and the Trinity. Also available as booklets.

A Life Worth Living   What happens after Alpha? Based on the book of Philippians, this is an invaluable next step for those who have just completed the Alpha course, and for anyone eager to put their faith on firm biblical footing.

How to Run the Alpha Course: Telling Others   The theological principles and the practical details of how courses are run. Each alternate chapter consists of a testimony of someone whose life has been changed by God through an Alpha course.

Challenging Lifestyle   Studies in the Sermon on the Mount showing how Jesus' teaching flies in the face of modern lifestyle and presents us with a radical alternative.

The Heart of Revival   Ten Bible studies based on the book of Isaiah, drawing out important truths for today by interpreting some of the teaching of the Old Testament prophet Isaiah. The book seeks to understand what revival might mean and how we can prepare to be part of it.

30 Days   Nicky Gumbel selects thirty passages from the Old and New Testament which can be read over thirty days. It is designed for those on an Alpha course and others who are interested in beginning to explore the Bible.

Why Jesus?   A booklet – given to all participants at the start of the Alpha course. 'The clearest, best illustrated and most challenging short presentation of Jesus that I know.' – Michael Green

All titles are by Nicky Gumbel, who is on the staff of Holy Trinity Brompton